SCHOLASTIC

Great GLYPHS

Holidays & Seasons

12 Skill-Building Activities That Motivate Kids to Collect, Display, and Use Data—and Connect to the NCTM Standards

by Patricia Daly and Teresa Cornell

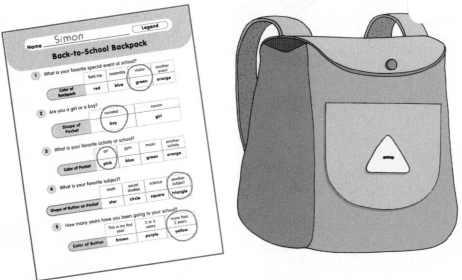

NEW YORK • TORONTO • LONDON • AUCKLAND • SYDNEY
MEXICO CITY • NEW DELHI • HONG KONG • BUENOS AIRES

Teaching *Resources*

To my husband Peter—Thank you for your love, respect, and support.
—P. D.

To Eli,
You add so much life to my life! I love you, Mommy.
—T. C.

Edited by Immacula A. Rhodes
Cover design by Maria Lilja and Norma Ortiz
Interior design by Holly Grundon
Cover and interior illustrations by Maxie Chambliss

ISBN: 0-439-41432-6
Copyright © 2006 by Patricia Daly and Teresa Cornell
Published by Scholastic Inc.
All rights reserved.
Printed in the U.S.A.

1 2 3 4 5 6 7 8 9 10   40   14 13 12 11 10 09 08 07 06

Once students have completed their glyphs, encourage them to make observations about their own glyphs and those of their classmates. Invite them to discuss how their glyph is similar to or different from others. Have them note the attributes of a classmate's glyph and write about what they know about that person based on the glyph. See pages 8–9 for other ways to extend learning.

Introducing Glyphs to Students

These activities are designed for flexible use in the classroom. You might use the activities in any order, or create a glyph each month as part of your classroom routine. You might also use literature to introduce a glyph-making activity and generate interest in the particular topic. A list of related literature links is included for each glyph.

Each glyph in this book comes with reproducible templates. In advance, photocopy the pattern pages and legend and collect any other materials necessary for making the glyph. Review the directions and extension activities, and determine which of these you might use.

When you first introduce glyphs to students, begin by showing them a completed glyph. Then show them step-by-step how you used the legend to create the glyph. As you add each attribute to the glyph (such as the number of whiskers on the rabbit), ask students what this feature represents. It is important for students to make the connection that each attribute of the glyph represents information, or data.

One way to do this is by reproducing and distributing the legend page of each glyph activity. You can also copy the information onto a sheet of chart paper. Be sure to review the legend and the meaning of each feature with students before and after they create their own glyphs. For beginning readers, provide directions orally, one step at a time. You might show students how to use a blank sheet of paper to cover the legend steps. Sliding the paper down to reveal one step at a time will help students focus on reading small amounts of text.

Using Glyphs With English Language Learners

Students who repeatedly hear words in context are more likely to use them and understand their meaning. The activities in this book help give English language learners exposure to vocabulary such as geometry words (shape names, directionality and position words), measurement terms (months of the year, seasons, time), and number concepts (ordinality, cardinality, even and odd). Reviewing the directions and legend with students to introduce each activity and following up with a discussion and interpretation of the glyphs gives students even greater exposure to the vocabulary. As students compare the attributes of each glyph, they use number words, shape names, measurement terms, and more. This repeated exposure greatly benefits ELL students.

A Teacher-Student Dialogue

The following is an example of a classroom dialogue introducing glyphs to students for the first time. For each new glyph, modify the discussion to focus on the questions asked in the glyph-making activities and the responses students represent in their glyph. As you ask students questions, focus on mathematical concepts of the glyph rather than the craft-making aspect.

Teacher: (*holding up the completed backpack glyph so that the whole class can see it*) Children, look at this picture and think of something that you can say about what you see.

Student: It looks like a backpack with a pocket on it.

Student: There's a star on the pocket. It's a button.

Student: The pocket is blue, but the button is yellow.

Student: The backpack is a different color, too. It's green!

Teacher: All the attributes you just talked about tell something special about me. This backpack is a glyph. A glyph tells information about the person who made it. Let's find out what that information is. (*Reveal the legend, one item at a time, pointing to each feature on the backpack glyph.*) The color of the backpack tells you about my favorite special event at school. The legend shows that if my favorite event is a field trip, the backpack is red. It is blue if my favorite event is an assembly, green if I enjoy a visitor most, and orange if I prefer another kind of event. What does the color of my backpack tell you about my favorite special event at school?

Student: It tells us that you like to have a visitor.

Teacher: Yes, I colored my backpack green because my favorite event is having visitors. Now let's look at the shape of the pocket. What does it tell us about me? Look at the legend and think about the information that you know about me based on the shape of the pocket.

Student: You used a round pocket. The legend shows that a rounded pocket means you are a boy.

Teacher: That's right. A girl will use a square pocket on her backpack, and a boy will use a rounded pocket. Now look at the color of the pocket. This will tell us my favorite activity at school. If the pocket is pink, it means I like art best. If the pocket is blue, it means I prefer gym. A green pocket means I like music best, and an orange pocket means another activity is my favorite. What is my favorite activity at school?

Student: You like gym the most.

Teacher: How did you know that?

Student: Your pocket is blue, and a blue pocket means that gym is your favorite activity at school.

Teacher: What about the button on the pocket? What does it tell us about my favorite subject? The legend shows that if my favorite subject is math, the button will be a star. If my favorite subject is social studies, it will be a circle. A square button means that my favorite subject is science. A triangle button means that another subject is my favorite. What is the shape of my button?

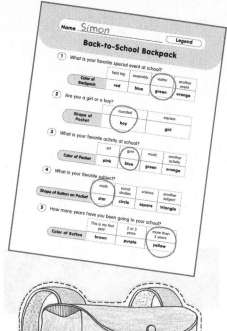

Student: It is a star. That means your favorite subject is math.

Teacher: How do you know that my favorite subject is not science or social studies?

Student: If your favorite subject was science, then your button would be square. It would be a circle if you liked social studies best.

Teacher: You're right! Now look at the color of the button to see how many years I've been at this school. A brown button means that this is my first year at this school. If the button is purple, I have been at this school for two or three years. A yellow button means that I have been at this school for more than three years. How long have I been at this school?

Student: Your button is yellow. You've been at this school for more than three years.

Teacher: Yes, that's true. Now, let's review everything you know about me so far, based on the glyph I've made. *(Discuss the legend and have students tell what they have learned.)* Remember that when you are trying to get information from a glyph, the legend reminds you what each part of the glyph represents. Now each of you will make glyphs about yourselves.

Making Glyphs With Students

After you have shown students an example of a completed glyph and reviewed the legend with them, begin by asking them to complete the first question on the legend. Remind students what information this attribute on the glyph will reveal. Wait for students to color, cut, and paste to complete the first question. Then hold up several glyphs in progress, one at a time, and ask the class to explain what each glyph tells so far about the child who made it. If you do this each time a new attribute is added, students will begin to grasp the concept that the attributes represent data. This also gives students a chance to practice analyzing the data shown on the glyph.

To make a glyph activity a rich and meaningful mathematics experience, rather than an arts and crafts project, encourage children to carefully consider each item on the legend before they select and add that attribute to their glyph. Remind students that each feature on their glyph should represent something about themselves—based on the legend.

Once the Glyph Is Complete— Extending Learning

Taking time to analyze the glyphs gives students a rich opportunity to build key math skills. For each glyph, you will find suggestions for critical-thinking activities and other extension activities that connect glyph-making to math concepts and to other areas of the curriculum. You will also find suggestions for books that explore the same themes as the glyphs. Use these to introduce or wrap up a glyph-making activity.

When students have completed their first glyph activity, ask them to work with a partner. Have each pair exchange their glyphs and tell a larger group or the whole class what they know about their partner based on the glyph. Older students can write these descriptions and then give them to their partner to read. As they talk and write, students are interpreting and analyzing data.

Another follow-up activity is to brainstorm ways to sort the completed glyphs. Divide the class into small groups and have each group determine how they will sort their glyphs. For example, they might sort the Summer's Here! glyphs by the number of shells or by the color of the sand pail. As each group reports to the class, ask them to show the sorting method, and then discuss the data that is revealed by each way of sorting. Since each glyph has many different attributes, each can be sorted in a variety of ways. Keeping the glyphs sorted, display them on a bulletin board with the question "How did we sort our glyphs?" Invite students from other classrooms to interpret the data.

With any glyph activity, students can write a story or poem, draw or write about their glyph and their findings in their math journals, or extend the glyph with other symbols to represent additional information.

Feel free to modify elements of the glyphs as needed to make them more appropriate for your students. We have found these activities highly motivating to students—and students' use of mathematics vocabulary improves as they create glyphs and interpret the data revealed in them. Enjoy!

Connections to the NCTM Standards

The activities in this book correspond to the standards recommended by the National Council of Teachers of Mathematics (NCTM).

Glyph Activity	Content Standards					Process Standards				
	Number and Operations	Algebra	Geometry	Measurement	Data Analysis and Probability	Problem Solving	Reasoning and Proof	Communication	Connections	Representation
September **Back-to-School Backpack**	●		●		●	●	●	●	●	●
October **Autumn Tree**			●		●	●	●	●	●	●
November **Thanksgiving Feast**	●		●	●	●	●	●	●	●	●
December **Holiday Lights**	●			●	●	●	●	●	●	●
January **New Year's Party Hat**	●			●	●	●	●	●	●	●
February **Message From the Heart**	●	●	●		●	●	●	●	●	●
March **Hippity-Hoppity Rabbit**	●		●		●	●	●	●	●	●
April **Let's Learn About Earth**	●				●	●	●	●	●	●
May **My Very Own Butterfly**				●	●	●	●	●	●	●
June **Flag Day Fun**	●	●	●		●	●	●	●	●	●
July **Pack Your Suitcase!**	●	●		●	●	●	●	●	●	●
August **Summer's Here!**	●		●		●	●	●	●	●	●

Back-to-School Backpack

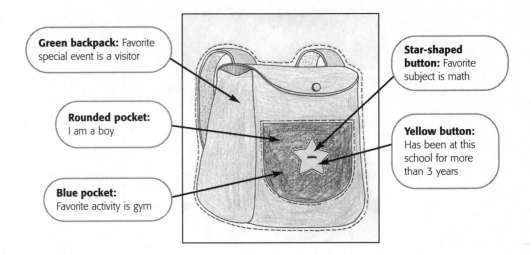

Green backpack: Favorite special event is a visitor

Rounded pocket: I am a boy

Blue pocket: Favorite activity is gym

Star-shaped button: Favorite subject is math

Yellow button: Has been at this school for more than 3 years

Math Skills

- geometry: shapes
- counting
- greater than

Materials

- reproducible glyph patterns and legend (pages 12–14)
- completed backpack glyph
- scissors
- glue or paste
- crayons

Creating the Glyph

Distribute copies of the back-to-school backpack glyph patterns and legend to students. Review the legend, one characteristic at a time, as you display a glyph you have completed. Then distribute the other materials, and invite students to use the legend to create their own personal backpack glyph.

Critical Thinking

Ask students whether they think more boys or girls prefer field trips. After they make their predictions, work with students to create a method that will help answer the question. Encourage them to use the same method to answer whether more boys or girls prefer other school events, such as assemblies and visitors.

One method students might use is to place two large string circles or hula hoops on the floor. Label one circle "Boys" and the other "Girls." Have each student place his or her glyph in one circle or the other. Then ask students to eliminate all the glyphs that do not help answer the question. (In this case, keep only the red glyphs. These are the students whose favorite special event is a field trip.) Afterward, have children discuss and interpret the results. Then they can count and compare the number of glyphs in each circle to discover whether more boys or girls prefer field trips.

Explore More

Math Challenge students to write number sentences to compare boys' and girls' preferences for different school events, activities, or subjects. For example, students might count the number of boys and the number of girls who prefer assemblies. Then have them write their findings in a number sentence using the signs for *greater than*, *less than*, or *equal to*.

Math Have ten students line up their backpacks or other book bags. Then invite small groups to choose an attribute by which to sort the backpacks. For example, students might sort the backpacks by whether or not they have side pockets. After the backpacks have been sorted, ask the rest of the class to look for the attribute all the backpacks in one group have in common.

Language Arts Invite students to cut out a copy of the backpack pattern on page 13. Then have them trace the outline on several plain sheets of paper and cut out the shapes. To make booklets, ask students to draw a different school item on each blank page. They might draw a crayon, ruler, and eraser, each on a separate page. After illustrating each page, have students write about how they use that item in school. Next, help students stack and staple their pages to the backpack cutout. Finally, have them write a title on the backpack cover and then decorate it with designs and colors of their choice.

Social Studies Have students research and learn about the different jobs people do in your school. Invite pairs of students to choose someone in the school to interview (principal, nurse, custodian, and so on). In advance, have students write a list of questions to ask. Encourage them to take notes during the interview and then report back what they learned to the rest of the class.

 **Literature Links**

First Day Jitters
by Julie Danneberg
(Charlesbridge, 2000).
A clever twist in text and illustrations leads readers to discover that even teachers get butterflies on the first day of school.

If You Take a Mouse to School
by Laura Joffe Numeroff
(Laura Geringer Books, 2002).
When a mouse asks to go to school, he also asks for a lunch box, then a sandwich, and then a snack for later. At school, he wants to participate in everything, including math and soccer. He even finds that spending time in a backpack can be lots of fun!

Back-to-School Backpack

1 What is your favorite special event at school?

	field trip	assembly	visitor	another event
Color of Backpack	**red**	**blue**	**green**	**orange**

2 Are you a girl or a boy?

	boy	girl
Shape of Pocket	**rounded**	**square**

3 What is your favorite activity at school?

	art	gym	music	another activity
Color of Pocket	**pink**	**blue**	**green**	**orange**

4 What is your favorite subject?

	math	social studies	science	another subject
Shape of Button on Pocket	**star**	**circle**	**square**	**triangle**

5 How many years have you been going to your school?

	This is my first year.	2 or 3 years	more than 3 years
Color of Button	**brown**	**purple**	**yellow**

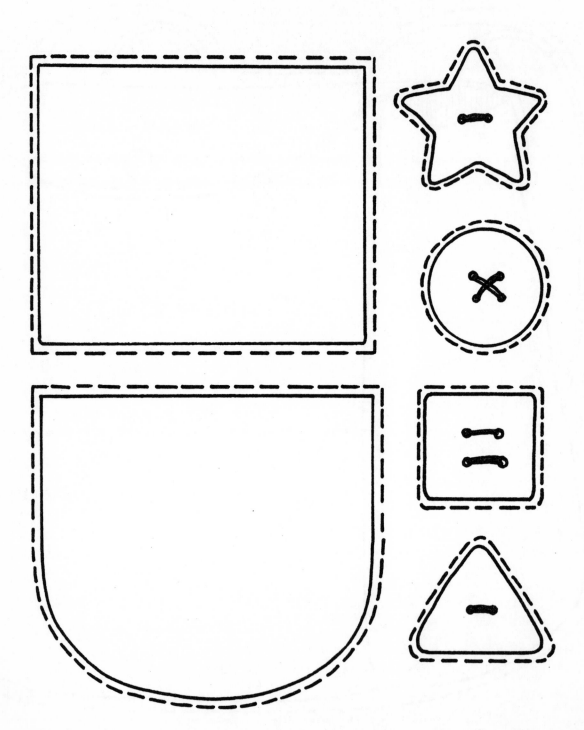

Autumn Tree

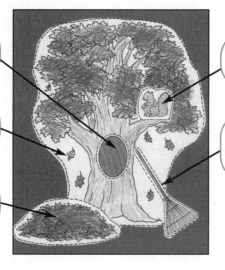

Large oval hole in trunk:
Favorite special day in fall is different than choices listed

Orange leaves:
Would rather play a sport in the fall

Large leaf pile: Would rather wear a sweater in cool weather

Squirrel on right:
Favorite color of fall leaves is yellow

Rake leaning on right side: Odd number of people in family

Creating the Glyph

Distribute copies of the autumn tree glyph patterns and legend to students. Review the legend, one characteristic at a time, as you display a glyph you have completed. Then distribute the other materials, and invite students to use the legend to create their own personal autumn tree glyph. Have students glue all the elements of the glyph onto a vertical sheet of construction paper, overlapping them slightly.

Critical Thinking

Use students' glyphs to create logic problems. Give clues based on a glyph's features and then have students guess the glyph. For example:

> There is a medium pile of leaves.
> The leaves are brown.
> It has an oval hole.
> There is a squirrel on top of it.
> The rake is leaning on the right side.
> Which tree is it?

Or provide higher-order thinking problems by naming what each feature represents. For the same glyph above, you might give these clues:

> I like to wear a jacket in the fall.
> My favorite fall activity is picking apples.
> My favorite special day is Halloween.
> I like orange leaves the best.
> There is an odd number of people in my family.
> Which tree is mine?

Math Skills

- geometry: shapes
- size: small, medium, large
- directionality: top, bottom, left, right
- even and odd numbers

Materials

- reproducible glyph patterns and legend (pages 17–19)
- completed tree glyph
- 9- by 12-inch construction paper
- scissors
- glue or paste
- crayons

Explore More

Math Ask students to cut out five identical leaf shapes from fall colors of construction paper. To make a ruler with nonstandard units of measure, have them glue the leaves end to end on a strip of card stock. Invite students to use their leaf rulers to measure how many leaves wide the door is, how many leaves tall a bookshelf is, and so on.

Language Arts Invite students to write a poem about their favorite fall activity or special day. Encourage them to use a simple rhyming pattern such as AB/AB or AAB/AAB. Then have students illustrate their poems. After each student has had a chance to read his or her poem to the class, compile all the pages into a class poetry book. Place the book in the reading center for students to enjoy during free-choice reading time.

Science Have students research squirrels. Give students several copies of the squirrel pattern (page 19) to glue onto index cards. Have them write facts about squirrels on their cards. After students share their facts with the class, display the cards on a bulletin board—or use them in a shared writing activity to show students how to write a report.

Language Arts Ask students to write each letter of their favorite fall holiday on separate leaf cutouts. Challenge them to create new words using the letters on the leaves. Each time they make a word, have students write it on a sheet of paper. Later, group together students who have the same favorite special day. Invite group members to share and compare their list of words.

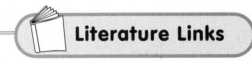 **Literature Links**

Red Leaf, Yellow Leaf
by Lois Ehlert
(Harcourt Brace Jovanovich, 1991).
Bright vivid colors illustrate a maple tree's growth from seedling to an adult tree with its glorious canopy of red and gold leaves. Tree facts and instructions on planting a tree are included in the back of the book.

Ska-tat!
by Kimberly Knutson
(Macmillan Publishing Company, 1993).
Three children enjoy a sensory adventure as they experience the many sights, sounds, and textures that accompany a tumble in the leaves.

Autumn Tree

1 Which would you rather wear in cool weather?

	sweatshirt	jacket	sweater
Size of Leaf Pile	**small**	**medium**	**large**

2 Which activity would you rather do in the fall?

	play a sport	pick apples	go the playground	another activity
Color of Leaves	**orange**	**brown**	**red**	**yellow**

3 What special day in the fall do you enjoy most?

	Labor Day	Halloween	Thanksgiving	another day
Shape of Hole in Tree Trunk	**small circle**	**large circle**	**small oval**	**large oval**

4 What color fall leaves do you like best?

	orange	brown	red	yellow
Position of Squirrel	**top of tree**	**bottom of tree**	**left side of tree**	**right side of tree**

5 Do you have an odd or even number of people in your family?

	odd	even
Position of Rake Leaning Against Tree	**on the right side**	**on the left side**

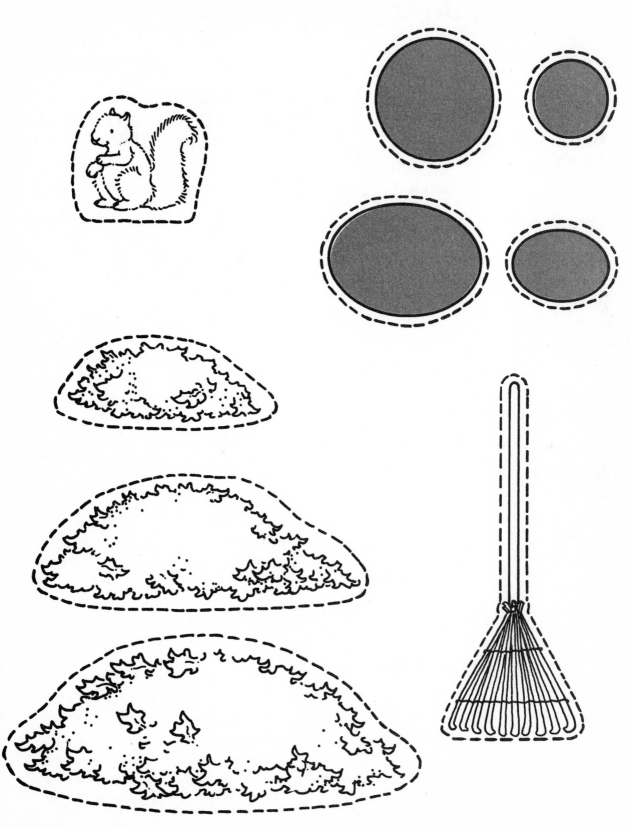

Thanksgiving Feast

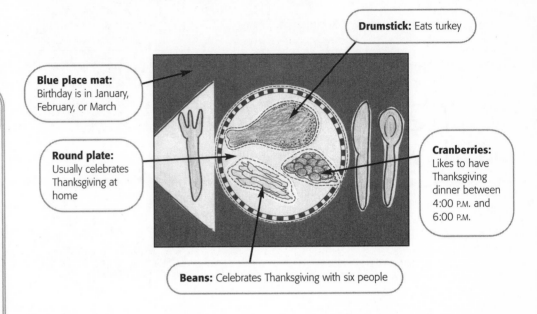

Drumstick: Eats turkey

Blue place mat: Birthday is in January, February, or March

Round plate: Usually celebrates Thanksgiving at home

Cranberries: Likes to have Thanksgiving dinner between 4:00 P.M. and 6:00 P.M.

Beans: Celebrates Thanksgiving with six people

Math Skills

- geometry: shapes

- time concepts: months of the year, A.M./P.M.

- counting

- greater than, less than, equal to

Materials

- reproducible glyph patterns and legend (pages 22–24)

- completed Thanksgiving feast glyph

- 9- by 12-inch blue, orange, red, and green construction paper

- scissors

- glue or paste

- crayons

Creating the Glyph

1. Distribute copies of the Thanksgiving feast glyph patterns and legend to students. Review the legend one characteristic at a time, as you display a glyph you have completed. Then distribute the other materials and invite students to use the legend to create their own personal Thanksgiving feast glyph.

2. Have students choose the color of construction paper that corresponds to their answer to question 1. (Students will use this piece, positioned horizontally, for a place mat.) Have students glue or tape the plate pattern to the place mat.

3. Invite students to glue on a folded napkin and utensils cut from paper.

Critical Thinking

Ask students which feature of the Thanksgiving feast glyph they would look at to identify in which month their classmates were born (*the color of the place mat*). Gather students' ideas about how they could make a graph that would represent this information. Then divide the class into small groups. Ask some groups to make a vertical bar graph and the others to make a horizontal bar graph. When finished, discuss with students how both types represent the same data.

Explore More

Math   Invite students to bring in recipes for their favorite Thanksgiving foods. As each student shares his or her recipe with the class, ask specific math-related questions about the recipe. (You might want to display a set of measuring tools for students to refer to.) For example, you might ask: "Does the recipe have any measurements written as fractions?" and "Which ingredient is needed in the largest quantity?" If the recipe is for a food that needs to be baked, name a time, such as 1:30 P.M. Then ask students to tell at what time the baking will be finished. To further challenge students, ask them to divide the quantity for a specific ingredient in half or double a given quantity.

Social Studies   Help students research the first Thanksgiving to learn what kinds of food were available to Pilgrims at the time. A good resource is *Eating the Plates: A Pilgrim Book of Food and Manners*, by Lucille Recht Penner (Macmillan, 1992). Once students have generated a list of Pilgrim foods, ask them to list foods that they have for Thanksgiving dinner. Then have them create a Venn diagram to compare the foods eaten at that first Thanksgiving to some of the foods eaten today. How are the foods similar and different?

Science   Using the lists of foods generated in the social studies activity above, have students sort the foods into the following food groups: grains; vegetables; fruits; milk, yogurt, and cheese; and meat, beans, eggs, and nuts. Small groups can create one poster categorizing foods from the first Thanksgiving and a separate posterboard for foods from a modern-day Thanksgiving. When finished, have them compare the two posters to find similarities and differences.

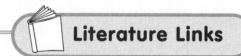
Literature Links

If You Were at the First Thanksgiving
by Anne Kamma (Scholastic, 2001).
This book provides information about the first Thanksgiving in a question-and-answer format.

Thanksgiving at the Tappleton's
by Eileen Spinelli (Addison-Wesley, 1982).
On Thanksgiving Day, everyone has a job to help Mrs. Tappleton prepare dinner. However, one problem after another arises and threatens the success of the dinner.

'Twas the Night Before Thanksgiving
by Dav Pilkey
(Orchard Books, 1990).
Eight schoolchildren take a field trip to a turkey farm just before Thanksgiving. When the children learn about the turkeys' fate, they devise a plan to save their feathered friends from Farmer MacNugget's ax.

Thanksgiving Feast

1 Thanksgiving falls in November. In which month is your birthday?

	January, February, or March	April, May, or June	July, August, or September	October, November, or December
Color of Place Mat	blue	orange	red	green

2 Where do you usually celebrate Thanksgiving?

	at home	away from home
Shape of Plate	circle	oval

3 Do you eat turkey?

	yes	no
Type of Main Dish	drumstick	casserole

4 With how many other people do you celebrate Thanksgiving?

	more than 6	fewer than 6	exactly 6
Type of Vegetable	corn	broccoli	beans

5 At what time do you like to have dinner on Thanksgiving?

	before 4:00 P.M.	between 4:00 P.M. and 6:00 P.M.	after 6:00 P.M.
Type of Side Dish	roll	cranberries	stuffing

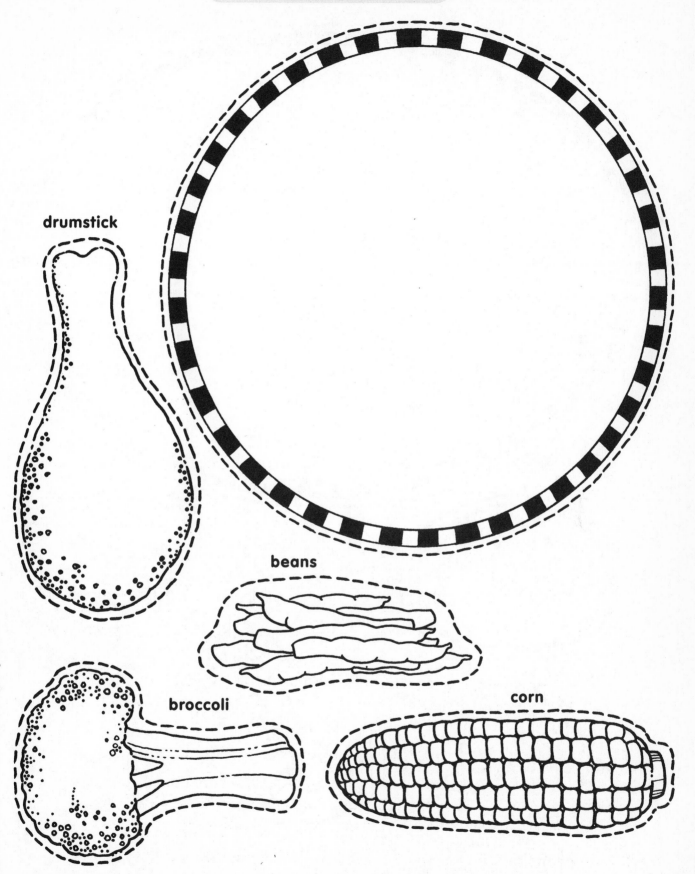

drumstick

beans

broccoli

corn

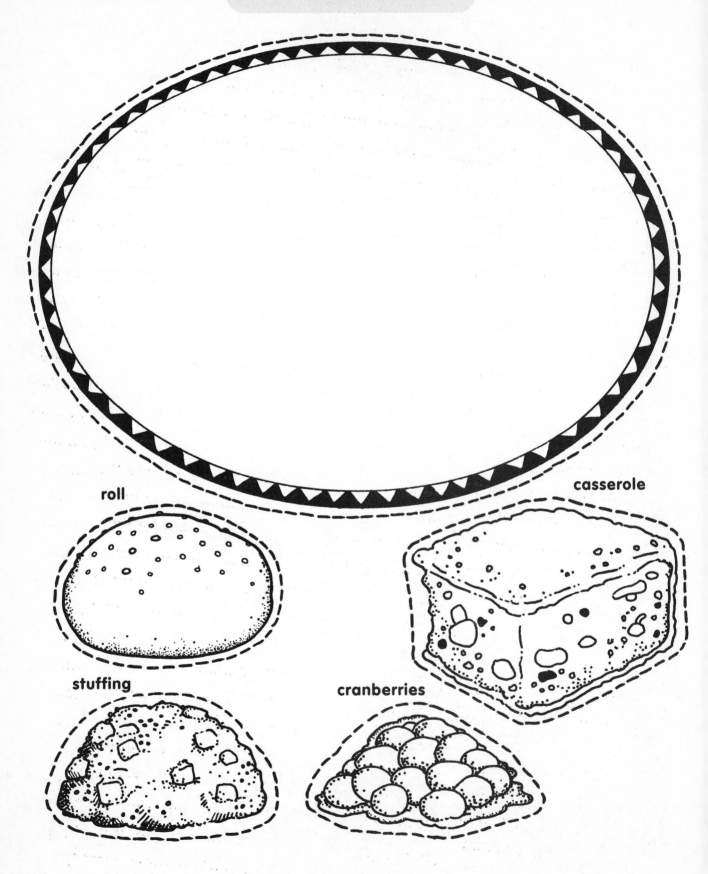

roll

casserole

stuffing

cranberries

Holiday Lights

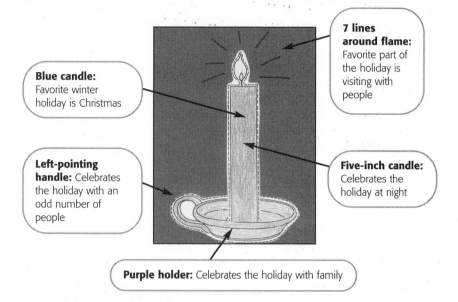

Blue candle: Favorite winter holiday is Christmas

7 lines around flame: Favorite part of the holiday is visiting with people

Left-pointing handle: Celebrates the holiday with an odd number of people

Five-inch candle: Celebrates the holiday at night

Purple holder: Celebrates the holiday with family

Creating the Glyph

1. Distribute copies of the candle glyph patterns and legend to students. Review the legend, one characteristic at a time, as you display a glyph you have completed. Then distribute the other materials and invite students to use the legend to create their own personal candle glyph.

2. For question 2, have students use rulers to measure their candle and cut it to the length that matches their answer. Instruct them to measure from the tip of the candle (not including the wick or flame) to the bottom.

3. As they complete question 3, have students glue their candle and holder onto a sheet of vertical construction paper for a sturdy backing.

4. For question 5, have students draw short lines radiating from the flame.

Critical Thinking

Play a game of Ten Questions with the class. Post 6–8 glyphs on a bulletin board or wall. Invite a volunteer to choose a glyph and whisper his or her choice to you. Then have classmates take turns asking questions about the characteristics of the "secret" glyph. They may ask only questions that can be answered with a simple yes or no. For example, they might ask, "Does the glyph show that the person's favorite winter holiday is Hanukkah?" "Does the person

Math Skills

● measurement: length

● counting

● directionality: left, right

● odd and even numbers

● one-to-one correspondence

● greater than, less than

Materials

● reproducible glyph patterns and legend (pages 27–28)

● completed candle glyph

● 9- by 12-inch construction paper

● 12-inch rulers

● scissors

● glue or paste

● crayons

celebrate during the day?" "Does the person celebrate with both family and friends?" After the student answers each question, have other students remove the glyphs that are eliminated from the running. Challenge students to identify the glyph in ten guesses or fewer.

Explore More

Math Wrap two small boxes and their lids separately in holiday gift wrap. Place an item in each box and close the lid. Then invite students to pick up and compare the weights of the boxes. Have them predict which box weighs more. After recording students' predictions, place a box on each side of a balance. Compare the results to find out which predictions were correct.

Math, Science Place an object in one of the wrapped boxes (see above activity). Then give students a collection of small wood cubes (or any other object that can be used for weights). Ask students to estimate how many cubes will equal the weight of the box. Afterward, invite them to place the box on one side of a balance and the wood cubes on the other side to balance the scale. Have them count the cubes and compare the results with their estimates. Were their estimates correct?

Social Studies, Language Arts Gather a selection of books about different winter holidays around the world. Encourage students to explore the books and choose one holiday to research in depth. Have students work with partners to research the holiday and record information. Then invite students to give short presentations to the class on what they learned about the holiday. Post a world map on the wall and point out the different places where each holiday is celebrated.

 **Literature Links**

Children Just Like Me: Celebrations
by Anabel Kindersley
(Dorling Kindersley, 1997).
Photo-illustrations feature children from all around the world celebrating different holidays. This is a good resource for learning about customs and festivities of various cultures.

Lights of Winter: Winter Celebrations Around the World
by Heather Conrad
(Lightport Books, 2001).
Simple, colorful illustrations highlight how ten different winter celebrations are observed and how they are similar to one another.

Holiday Lights

1 What is your favorite winter holiday?

	Hanukkah	Kwanzaa	Christmas	Las Posadas	another holiday
Color of Candle	red	yellow	blue	green	orange

2 When do celebrate your favorite winter holiday?

	during the day	at night	both day and night
Length of Candle	6 inches	5 inches	4 inches

3 With how many other people do you celebrate your favorite winter holiday?

	odd number of people	even number of people
Position of Handle on Holder	left	right

4 Do you celebrate your favorite winter holiday with family or friends?

	family	friends	both
Color of Holder	purple	pink	gray

5 What do you like most about your favorite winter holiday? Draw lines.

	eating food	listening to music	visiting with people	another activity
Number of Lines Around Flame	fewer than 4	more than 3 but fewer than 6	6 or 7	more than 7 but fewer than 10

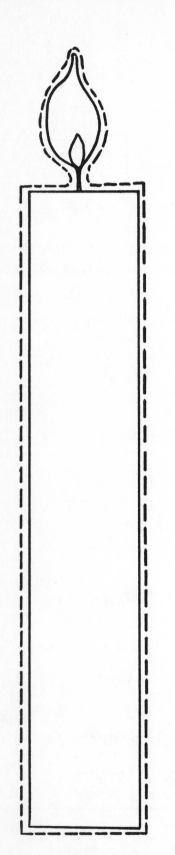

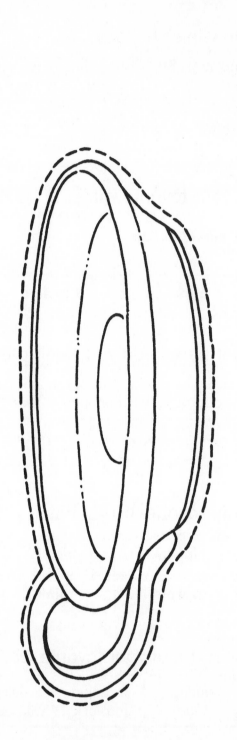

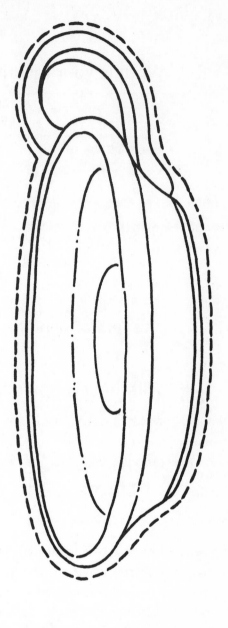

Great Glyphs: Holidays & Seasons Scholastic Teaching Resources

New Year's Party Hat

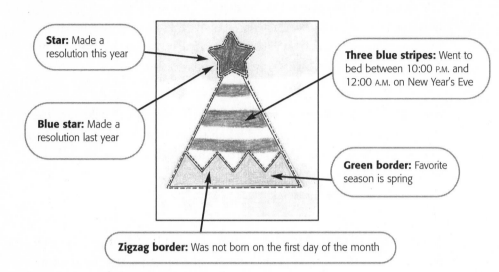

Star: Made a resolution this year

Blue star: Made a resolution last year

Three blue stripes: Went to bed between 10:00 P.M. and 12:00 A.M. on New Year's Eve

Green border: Favorite season is spring

Zigzag border: Was not born on the first day of the month

Creating the Glyph

Distribute copies of the party hat glyph patterns and legend to students. Review the legend, one characteristic at a time, as you display a glyph you have completed. Then distribute the other materials and invite students to use the legend to create their own personal party hat glyph.

Critical Thinking

Create a four-column chart on a length of bulletin board paper. Label each column with the name of a season. Then have students place their glyph in the column that corresponds to their favorite season. Invite students to use the chart to answer questions about different characteristics of the glyphs. You might ask questions, such as:

- *Which season is the favorite of the greatest number of people? The least number of people?*

- *Did more students who like fall the best make resolutions than the students who like winter best?*

- *How many people who like summer best were born on the first day of the month?*

- *Which group has the most people who went to bed after 12:00 A.M. on New Year's Eve?*

Math Skills

- ordinal numbers
- directionality: top
- time concepts: calendar, seasons, A.M./P.M.
- counting
- one-to-one correspondence

Materials

- reproducible glyph patterns and legend (pages 31–32)
- completed party hat glyph
- scissors
- glue or paste
- crayons

Explore More

Math At the beginning of each month, give students a blank calendar grid. Have them fill in the dates for the month as well as holidays, birthdays, and special events. Invite them to use their calendars to answer questions, such as "How many Mondays are in the month?" and "How many more days until Patricia's birthday?"

Social Studies Have students research New Year's celebrations of different cultures around the world. Pair up students and have each pair choose a country to research. After they have gathered and recorded information, let pairs present their findings to the class. Encourage students to compare the celebrations.

Social Studies, Math Display a large United States map that clearly shows the division of time zones across the country. (If the time zones are not marked, tape yarn from the top to the bottom of the map to mark the approximate locations of the time zone divisions.) Post a label with the name of each time zone above the corresponding section on the map: Eastern, Central, Mountain, and Pacific. Place a large, paper clock with movable hands above each zone.

Point to the time zone on the right—the Eastern time zone. Explain to students that when it is 12:00 Eastern time, the time in the zone to its west (Central time) is 11:00. Tell them that the time changes by one hour each time a person travels from one zone to the next. Then make up problems for students to solve using what they know about time zones. For example, you might ask, "If it is 11:00 A.M. in New York, what time is it in California?" Encourage students to move the clock hands and use A.M. and P.M. to express the times.

Literature Links

Happy New Year
by Emery Bernhard (Lodestar Books, 1996). Readers explore when and how different cultures around the world celebrate the new year. Information about the history and customs of the various celebrations keeps readers interested and engaged.

Happy New Year, Everywhere
by Arlene Erlbach (Millbrook Press, 2000). This introduction to New Year's celebrations in 20 countries describes each celebration and includes the dates, customs, and rituals associated with each. The author also provides directions for crafts, recipes, and activities related to the celebrations.

New Year's Party Hat

1 New Year's Day is the first day of January. Were you born on the first day of any month?

	yes	no
Shape of Border	∩∩∩∩∩∩	∧∧∧∧∧∧∧

2 People often set goals for the New Year called *resolutions*. Did you make a New Year's resolution this year?

	yes	no
Decoration on Top of Hat	star	pom-pom

3 Did you make a New Year's resolution last year?

	yes	no
Color of Star or Pom-pom	blue	orange

4 January is in the winter. What is your favorite season?

	winter	spring	summer	fall
Color of Border	purple	green	yellow	red

5 At what time did you go to bed on New Year's Eve?

	before 10:00 P.M.	between 10:00 P.M. and 12:00 A.M.	after 12:00 A.M.
Number of Blue Stripes on Hat	2 stripes	3 stripes	4 stripes

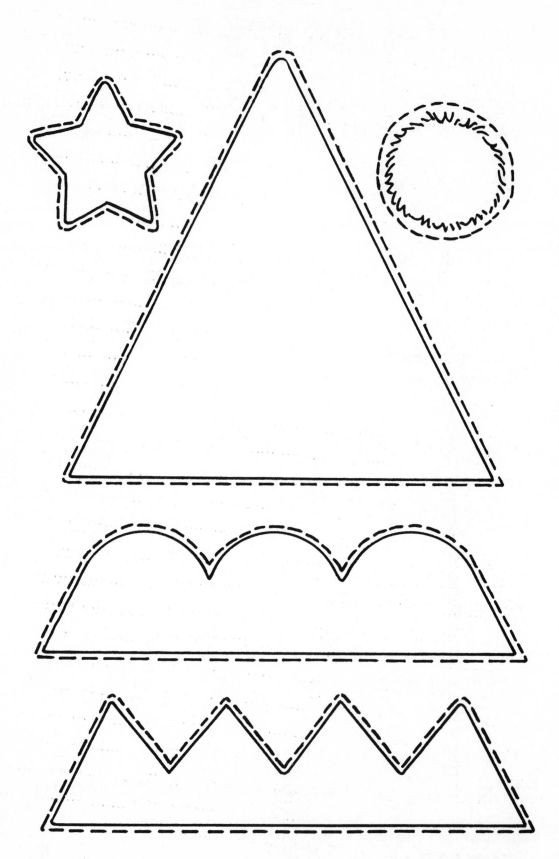

Great Glyphs: Holidays & Seasons Scholastic Teaching Resources

Message From the Heart

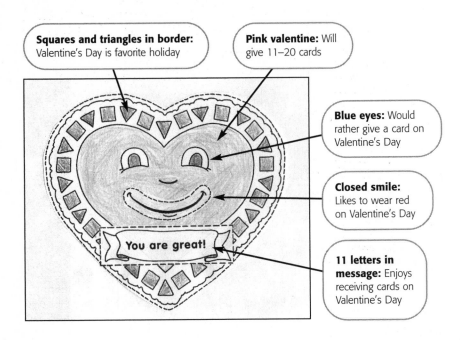

Squares and triangles in border: Valentine's Day is favorite holiday

Pink valentine: Will give 11–20 cards

Blue eyes: Would rather give a card on Valentine's Day

Closed smile: Likes to wear red on Valentine's Day

You are great!

11 letters in message: Enjoys receiving cards on Valentine's Day

Math Skills

- geometry: shapes
- patterns
- estimation
- counting
- greater than, less than, equal to

Creating the Glyph

1. Distribute copies of the valentine glyph patterns and legend to students. Review the legend, one characteristic at a time, as you display a glyph you have completed. Then distribute the other materials, and invite students to use the legend to create their own personal valentine glyph.

2. For question 5, have students glue a message across the bottom of the valentine.

Critical Thinking

Choose one attribute and arrange some of the completed valentine glyphs in an AB/AB pattern. For example, use the eyes and make a blue/brown/blue/brown pattern. Have students look at the glyphs and identify the pattern. Then ask them to select a valentine glyph that would come next to extend the pattern. Repeat the activity using another attribute to create another pattern, such as ABC/ABC.

Materials

- reproducible glyph patterns and legend (pages 35–37)
- completed valentine glyph
- scissors
- glue or paste
- crayons

33

Explore More

Math Cut out four heart shapes. Draw a circle, square, rectangle, and diamond, each on a separate heart. Then place the hearts in a paper bag, and have students conduct a probability experiment. Before starting, ask students to predict which shape they think will be pulled most often from the bag in 20 turns. Then have volunteers take turns pulling a heart from the bag, recording with tally marks the number of times each shape is pulled in 20 turns. (Return the heart to the bag after each turn.) Then continue the activity for 20 more turns. Did the results change after the last set of turns?

Language Arts Invite students to write a poem, using one or more of the messages on the glyphs. They might write the poem for a friend, family member, or even a pet. Encourage them to illustrate their poems.

Science, Math Have students place their hands on the middle of their chest to feel their heartbeat. Next, tell students that they can also "feel" their heartbeat in other places on their body: the wrist, neck, temple, and ankle. Have them find their pulse in each of these places. Then encourage students to choose one of these pulse points at which to take their pulse rate. Have them record their pulse rates for one minute at rest and again after a few minutes of vigorous exercise, such as running in place or doing jumping jacks. Ask them to compare their pulse rates for the two activities and then compute the difference in the number of heartbeats.

Literature Links

Guess How Much I Love You
by Sam McBratney
(Candlewick Press, 1995).
Little Nutbrown Hare's love for his father is as long as his arms can reach. His love is as high as the young hare can hop. Each time Little Nutbrown Hare expresses the extent of his love, Big Nutbrown Hare responds as only a loving parent can—with a wider, deeper, and more expansive love than can be measured.

Roses Are Pink, Your Feet Really Stink
by Diane de Groat
(Morrow Junior Books, 1996).
Gilbert finds himself in a dilemma when he anonymously writes not-so-nice valentine poems for two classmates—and gets caught!

Valentine's Day
by Gail Gibbons (Holiday House, 1986).
Colorful ink drawings and short text highlight history and customs related to Valentine's Day. Instructions for making a valentine card and box are included in the back of the book.

Message From the Heart

1 Is Valentine's Day your favorite holiday?

	yes	no
Border Around Heart	squares and triangles	circles and diamonds

2 How many cards will you give this Valentine's Day?

	10 or fewer cards	11–20 cards	21 or more cards
Color of Valentine	purple	pink	red

3 Which would you rather give to someone on Valentine's Day?

	a card	flowers	something else
Color of Eyes	blue	green	brown

4 Do you like to wear red on Valentine's Day?

	yes	no
Type of Smile	closed mouth	open mouth

5 What do you enjoy most about Valentine's Day?

	making cards	delivering cards	receiving cards	another activity
Number of Letters in Message	exactly 5	more than 5 but fewer than 10	more than 10 but fewer than 15	more than 15

You are great!

My Pal!

Great Glyphs: Holidays & Seasons   Scholastic Teaching Resources

My Friend!

Happy Valentine's Day!

Hippity-Hoppity Rabbit

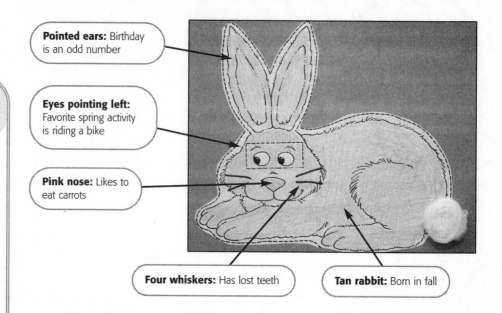

Pointed ears: Birthday is an odd number

Eyes pointing left: Favorite spring activity is riding a bike

Pink nose: Likes to eat carrots

Four whiskers: Has lost teeth

Tan rabbit: Born in fall

Math Skills

- even and odd numbers

- time concepts: seasons

- directionality: left, right, up, down

- counting

- one-to-one correspondence

Materials

- reproducible glyph patterns and legend (pages 40–42)

- completed rabbit glyph

- 9- by 12-inch construction paper

- scissors

- glue or paste

- crayons

- cotton balls

Creating the Glyph

Distribute copies of the rabbit glyph patterns and the legend to students. Review the legend, one characteristic at a time, as you display a glyph you have completed. Then distribute the other materials, and invite students to use the legend to create their own personal rabbit glyph. Have students glue the glyph onto construction paper for a sturdy backing. Invite them to add a cotton-ball tail to complete their glyph.

Critical Thinking

Select six of the completed rabbit glyphs and sort them into two groups. Ask students to guess the rule by looking for the attributes that are common to the rabbits in one of the groups. The attributes could be that all the rabbits have triangle ears (birthdays are on odd-numbered dates) and black noses (do not like carrots). For younger students, group glyphs by one attribute that is easy to identify. For older students, group the glyphs by more than one attribute and choose attributes that are less obvious.

Explore More

Math Reinforce measurement concepts with this movement activity. First, pair up students and clear a large, open area. Then have one child—the "bunny"—stand on a starting line. Ask the bunny to jump forward as far as

38

possible. Have the bunny's partner mark the spot where the bunny landed. Then, working together, the partners can measure the distance of the bunny's jump using nonstandard units, such as wood blocks or index cards. After they write the measurement in nonstandard units, have the pair measure the distance again, this time using standard measurement units, such as inches or feet. Once all the measurements have been recorded, have partners switch roles and repeat the activity. When finished, ask students to compare their results for the nonstandard and standard units of measure.

Science
Explain to students that there is a difference between rabbits and hares. Divide the class into two groups. Have one group research rabbits and the other research hares. As they work, encourage the groups to write on separate index cards each fact that they discover about their assigned animals. When finished, have the groups compare the similarities and differences between the two animals. They might do this by overlapping two large yarn circles on the floor to create a Venn diagram. Label one circle "Rabbits," the other circle "Hares," and the overlapping section "Both." Then have students place each fact card in the appropriate section of the diagram.

Language Arts
Have students write a story about what they think happened to a lost tooth (it could be their own or an imaginary character's). Where was the lost tooth placed? Did anyone retrieve the lost tooth? What happened to the person who lost the tooth? Encourage them to use their imagination and create a playful and engaging story that includes lots of dialogue and action.

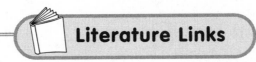

Literature Links

Hopper Hunts for Spring
by Marcus Pfister
(North-South Books, 1992).
When Hopper's mother tells her young hare that spring is coming, he sets off to meet what he hopes will be a new playmate. Although Hopper's search didn't turn up a friend named Spring, he does befriend a bear who has awakened from a long winter sleep.

Little Rabbit's Loose Tooth
by Lucy Bate (Crown Publishers, 1975).
When a little rabbit experiences the loss of her first tooth, she wonders if the tooth fairy really will come.

Rabbits and Raindrops
by Jim Arnosky (Putnam, 1997).
Five baby rabbits experience spring for the first time with their mother. After taking cover during a spring rain shower, the little bunnies are off again, eager to explore the world.

Hippity-Hoppity Rabbit

1 Is the date of your birthday an odd or even number?

	odd	even
Shape of Ears	pointed	rounded

2 Rabbits like to eat carrots. Do you like carrots?

	yes	no	I don't know.
Color of Nose	pink	black	red

3 In which season were you born?

	spring	summer	fall	winter
Color of Rabbit	white	yellow	tan	gray

4 Which activity do you enjoy most in the spring?

	flying a kite	playing sports	riding a bike	another activity
Direction of Eyes	up	down	left	right

5 Rabbits have four large front teeth. Have you lost any teeth? Draw whiskers.

	yes	no	No, but I have a loose tooth.
Number of Whiskers	4 whiskers	6 whiskers	8 whiskers

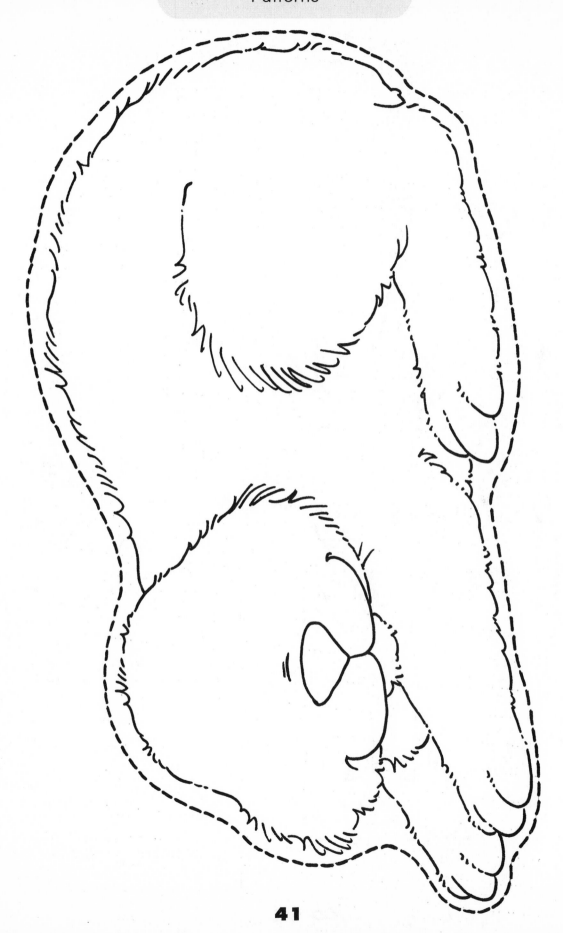

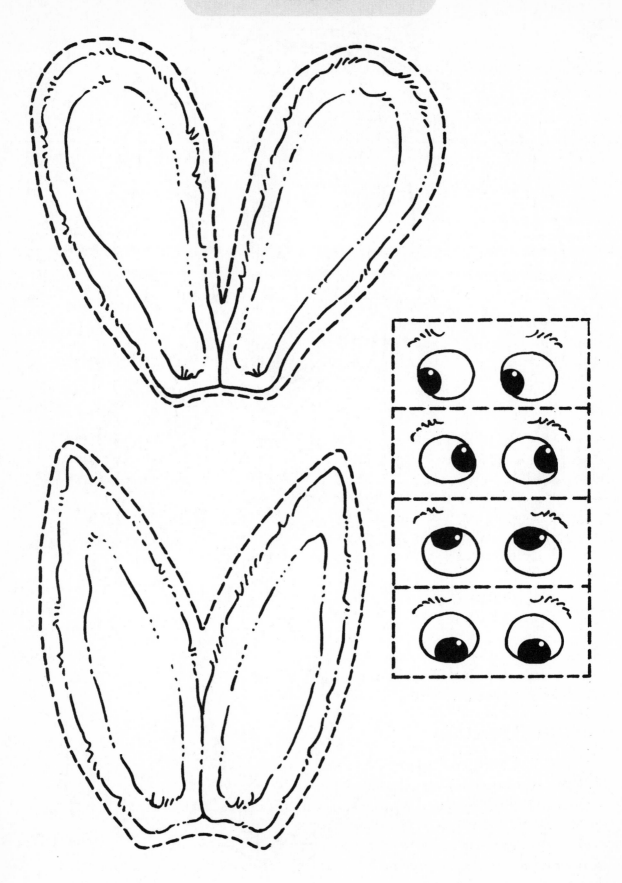

Let's Learn About Earth

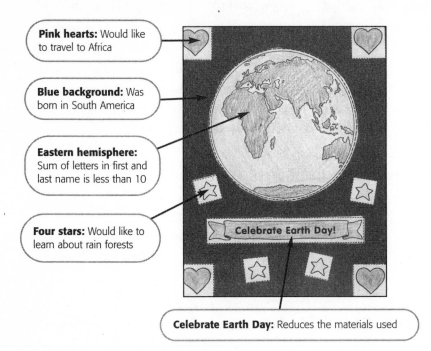

Pink hearts: Would like to travel to Africa

Blue background: Was born in South America

Eastern hemisphere: Sum of letters in first and last name is less than 10

Four stars: Would like to learn about rain forests

Celebrate Earth Day!

Celebrate Earth Day: Reduces the materials used

Math Skills

- greater than, less than
- counting
- one-to-one correspondence
- addition

Creating the Glyph

1. Distribute copies of the Earth patterns and legend to students. Review the legend, one characteristic at a time, as you display a completed glyph. Then distribute the other materials, and invite students to use the legend to create their own personal Earth glyph.

2. For question 1, have students choose the color of construction paper that corresponds to their answer, or color a sheet of white paper.

3. Have students position the construction paper vertically; then have them glue Earth to the center of the sheet, the four hearts in the corners, the stars around Earth, and the banner below Earth.

Critical Thinking

Ask students to sequence the glyphs by the number of stars. Then have them examine groups of glyphs with the same number of stars to find out what features they have in common. As students share their findings, ask them to tell what the similar features mean. For example, if glyphs have three stars and show the Eastern hemisphere, these students would like to learn about the desert and have fewer than ten letters in their first and last name combined.

Materials

- reproducible glyph pattern and legend (pages 45–47)
- completed Earth glyph
- 9- by 12-inch red, blue, green, yellow, purple, pink, and tan construction paper
- scissors
- glue or paste
- crayons

43

Explore More

Math   For this activity, you'll need large caps (rinsed clean) from liquid laundry detergent and clean, empty plastic bottles of different sizes and shapes. Have students choose two bottles that differ in size or shape. Invite them to predict how many capfuls of water will be needed to fill each one. Then have them fill the bottles with water, one cap at a time. When finished, let students compare the actual number of capfuls to their predictions. Then recycle the containers!

Science, Language Arts   Divide the class into groups according to which habitat they would most like to learn about. Have each group work together to make a list of questions about the habitat; then research to find the answers. Let each group create a large poster with facts about the habitat. Encourage them to draw a picture of the habitat as well as the creatures that live there.

Science, Social Studies   Divide the class into three groups, according to their responses to question 5 on their glyphs. Invite each group to list specific ways they protect Earth most often (by reducing the amount of materials they use, recycling, or reusing materials). For example, students might reduce the amount of paper towels they use at home by using a cloth hand towel instead. Have each group write their list on chart paper. Display the charts to encourage students to protect Earth.

 Literature Links

The Great Trash Bash
by Loreen Leedy (Holiday House, 1991).
When Mayor Hippo discovers that Beaston has too much trash, the townspeople start a cleanup and recycling campaign.

The Lorax
by Dr. Seuss (Random House, 1971).
In spite of warnings from the Lorax, the enterprising Once-ler strips the land of its natural resources to satisfy his own greed. Is the endangered land doomed to destruction?

Where Does the Garbage Go?
(Let's-Read-and-Find-Out Science 2)
by Paul Showers (HarperCollins, 1994).
Children take a field trip to a landfill to find out where the garbage goes and what happens to it when it gets there. Along the way, they learn how trash can be converted to energy and how paper, glass, and plastic are recycled.

Let's Learn About Earth

1 In which continent were you born?

	North America	South America	Asia	Africa	Europe	Australia	Antarctica
Color of Background	red	blue	green	yellow	purple	pink	tan

2 Add the number of letters in your first and last name. What is the sum?

	less than 10 letters	10 or more letters
Hemisphere	Eastern Hemisphere	Western Hemisphere

3 In which continent would you most like to travel?

	North America	South America	Asia	Africa	Europe	Australia	Antarctica
Color of Hearts	yellow	tan	purple	pink	green	red	blue

4 Which type of place would you like to learn about?

	desert	rain forest	coniferous forest	polar region	grassland	mountain
Number of Stars	3	4	5	6	7	8

5 Which do you do most often to protect the Earth?

	I reduce the materials I use.	I recycle materials.	I reuse materials.
Message Below Earth	Celebrate Earth Day!	Protect the Earth!	Conserve Resources!

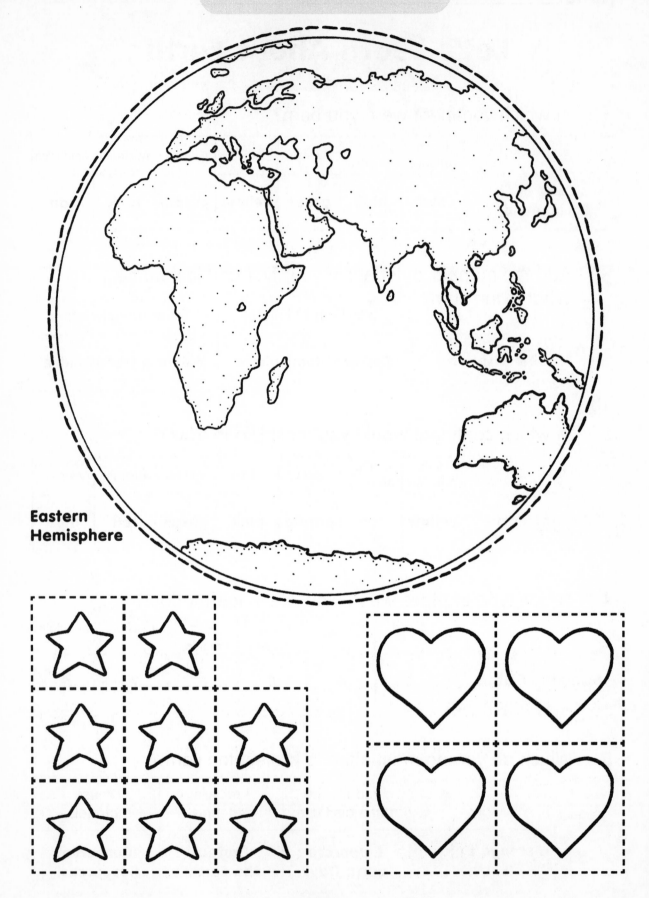

**Eastern
Hemisphere**

Western Hemisphere

Celebrate Earth Day!

Protect the Earth!

Conserve Resources!

My Very Own Butterfly

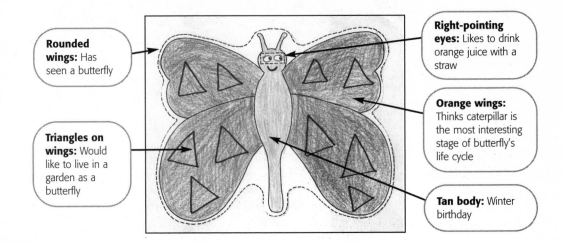

Rounded wings: Has seen a butterfly

Right-pointing eyes: Likes to drink orange juice with a straw

Triangles on wings: Would like to live in a garden as a butterfly

Orange wings: Thinks caterpillar is the most interesting stage of butterfly's life cycle

Tan body: Winter birthday

Math Skills

- geometry: shapes
- time concepts: seasons of the year
- directionality: left, right, up, down

Materials

- reproducible glyph patterns and legend (pages 50–52)
- completed butterfly glyph
- scissors
- crayons
- glue or paste

Creating the Glyph

Distribute copies of the butterfly glyph patterns and the legend to students. Review the legend, one characteristic at a time, as you display a glyph you have completed. Then distribute the other materials, and invite students to use the legend to create their own personal butterfly glyph.

Critical Thinking

Display all the glyphs. Have students sort the glyphs by wing color. When finished, ask students to identify the glyphs that belong to students who think the first stage of a butterfly's growth is most interesting (glyphs with yellow wings). Place these glyphs in a group and invite students to interpret the data represented on them. Challenge students to find glyphs in the group with other similarities—for example, yellow wings and eyes looking up. Group the rest of the glyphs by the different stages in question 3 (caterpillar, chrysalis, and butterfly) and have students interpret the data in each group.

Explore More

Math, Critical Thinking Have students work in pairs to create symmetrical butterflies with pattern blocks. To begin, give each student a copy of one of the butterfly patterns. Ask students to design a pattern on the left wing of their butterfly. Then have partners switch butterflies and challenge them to create a symmetrical pattern on the right wing.

Science   Share a book about butterflies with students to learn about the stages of a butterfly's development (see Literature Links). Afterward, have students illustrate and write about each stage of growth on a separate sheet of paper. When finished, ask them to sequence their pages, number each one, and then staple them together. To use, describe something that happens during one of the growth stages of a butterfly, such as "During this stage, the caterpillar stretches out of its old skin." Encourage students to refer to their pages to determine the stage at which the event happens and then identify the stage using ordinal numbers (first stage, second stage, and so on).

Science, Language Arts   Obtain a butterfly kit. As a class, follow the directions in the kit to grow a butterfly. As students observe the growth stages of a butterfly, have them record their observations in a journal. Once the butterflies have emerged, invite students to watch as you release the butterflies outdoors. Then hold a celebration to commemorate this special event!

Science, Music   Invite students to share in a song what they know about butterflies. First, list the titles of some familiar tunes on chart paper. Have students work with a partner to choose a song from the list. Then have them compose a song about butterflies, fitting the verse and rhythm to the meter of the song. Encourage students to include facts about a butterfly's development. After writing their songs, students can practice and then perform for the class.

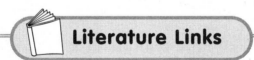

Literature Links

A Class Trip to Miss Hallberg's Butterfly Garden by Gay Bishop Brorstrom and Kathy Geotzel (Pipevine Press, 2000). On a class trip, children visit a butterfly garden and learn about this creature's life cycle.

Monarch Butterfly
by Gail Gibbons (Holiday House, 1989). Bright illustrations are combined with clearly written text to describe the life cycle, behavior, diet, and migration patterns of the monarch butterfly. Includes instructions on how to raise a butterfly.

Where Butterflies Grow
by Joanne Ryder (Lodestar Books, 1989). Readers imagine they are experiencing the amazing growth and transformation that take place as a caterpillar changes into a butterfly. Beautiful illustrations and many details add to the wonder.

My Very Own Butterfly

1 Have you ever seen a butterfly?

	yes	no
Shape of Wings		

2 If you were a butterfly, where would you like to live? Draw shapes on the wings.

	in a park	near a lake	in a garden	in another place
Shapes on Wings	☐	◯	△	⬭

3 What do you think is the most interesting stage of a butterfly's life cycle?

	egg	caterpillar	chrysalis	butterfly
Color of Wings	yellow	orange	pink	tan

4 Some butterflies emerge during the spring. In what season is your birthday?

	winter	spring	summer	fall
Color of Body	tan	pink	gray	purple

5 Butterflies drink with strawlike tongues. What do you most like to drink with a straw?

	apple juice	milk	orange juice	another beverage
Direction of Eyes				

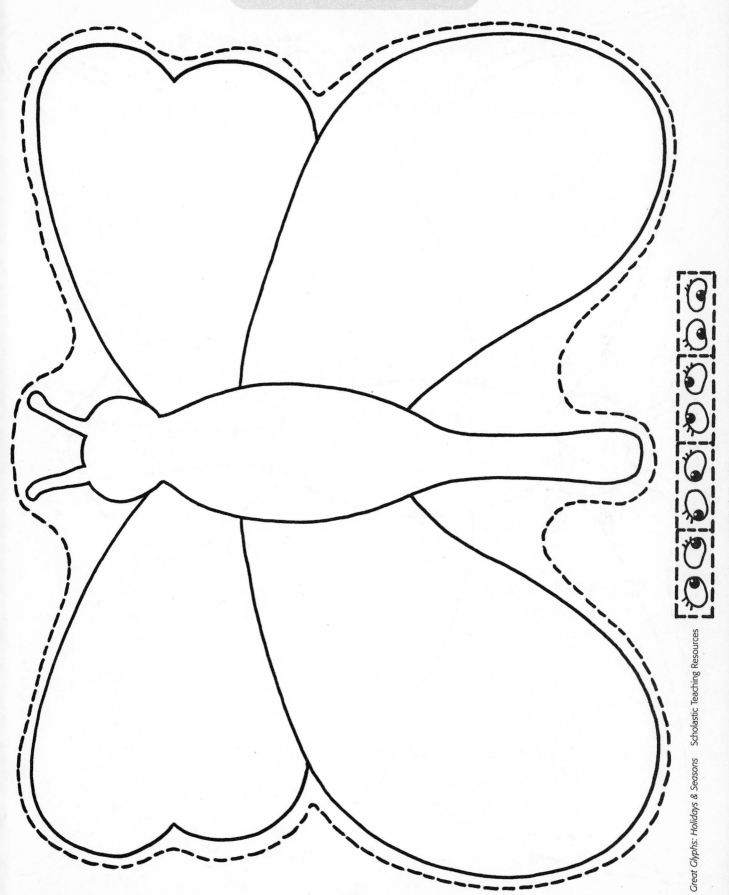

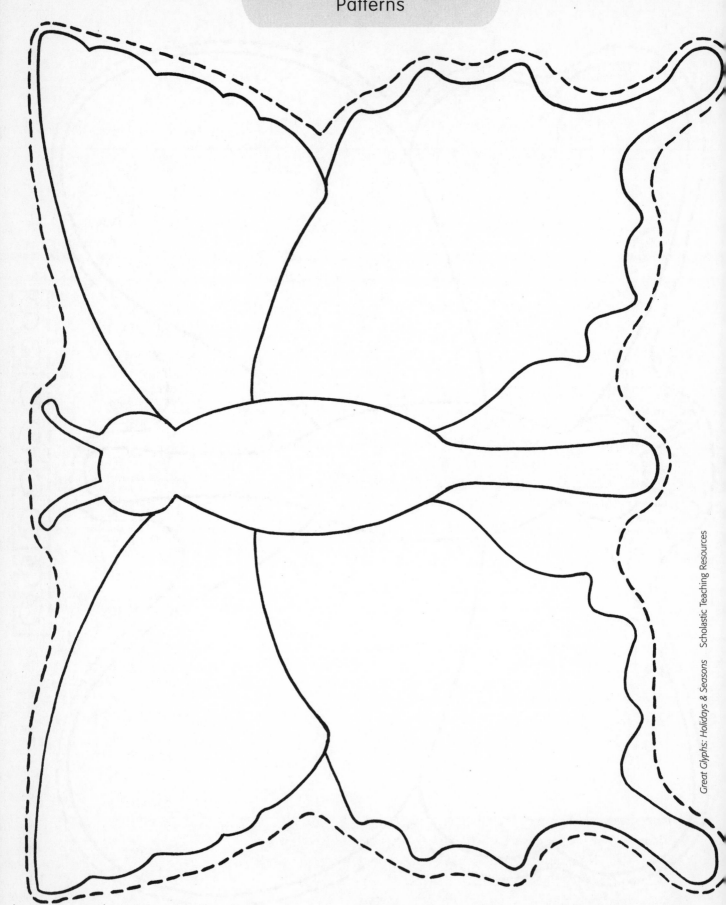

Flag Day Fun

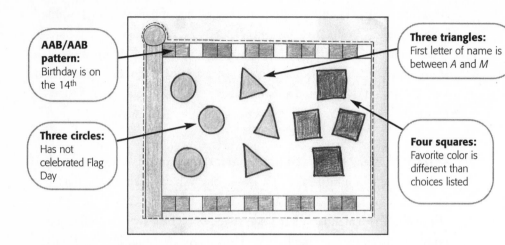

AAB/AAB pattern: Birthday is on the 14th

Three circles: Has not celebrated Flag Day

Three triangles: First letter of name is between *A* and *M*

Four squares: Favorite color is different than choices listed

Creating the Glyph

1. Distribute copies of the flag glyph patterns and the legend to students. Review the legend, one characteristic at a time, as you display a glyph you have completed. Then distribute the other materials, and invite students to use the legend to create their own personal flag glyph.

2. For questions 2, 3, and 4, have students draw the shapes in the center area of the flag. Have them draw lightly in pencil first so that they can make sure their shapes fit.

Critical Thinking

U se students' glyphs to generate logic problems. For example:

> *My birthday is after the 14th day of the month.*
> *I have celebrated Flag Day.*
> *The first letter of my name is between A and M.*
> *My favorite color is green or purple.*
> *Which flag is mine?*

Provide one clue at a time. After each clue is revealed, ask students which glyphs can be eliminated. Students can determine which glyph is correct through a process of elimination. Once you have modeled a few logic problems, invite volunteers to secretly choose a glyph and give clues to their classmates.

Math Skills

- patterns
- time concepts: dates
- geometry: shapes
- counting
- one-to-one correspondence
- odd and even numbers
- greater than, less than, equal to

Materials

- reproducible glyph patterns and legend (pages 55–56)
- completed flag glyph
- scissors
- crayons

53

Explore More

Math   Tell students that the American flag has seven red stripes and six white stripes. Then have them list on a sheet of paper all the possible ways to make 13 using two addends (12 + 1, 11 + 2, and so on). When finished, invite volunteers to take turns writing one of their answers on chart paper, making sure they don't repeat an answer that has already been listed. After all the possible answers have been listed, ask students to check their papers to see if they came up with all the answers.

Math   Display a calendar for the month of June. Ask students to find June 14. Explain June 14 is Flag Day—a day to pay tribute to the flag. Have students name the day of the week on which Flag Day falls. Then ask them other calendar-related questions, using Flag Day as a reference point. For example, you might ask, "How many days after Flag Day is the first day of summer?" "Is Flag Day the first, second, or third Wednesday of the month?" "How many days before Flag Day is the first Monday of the month?" and "What day of the week is the day before Flag Day?"

Art, Social Studies   Display an American flag or large photo of one. Invite students to use paint, crayons, or colored construction paper to create their own American flags. Then ask students to research Flag Day and the American flag's symbols and history. Have them record facts on index cards. After students share their flag facts with the class or with small groups, display the flags and facts in the hallway for visitors and other classes to enjoy.

 Literature Links

The Flag We Love
by Pamela Muñoz Ryan
(Charlesbridge Publishing, 1996).
This pictorial celebration of our national symbol includes many famous moments in United States history.

The Pledge of Allegiance (Scholastic, 2000).
Photographs of American landscapes, monuments, and flags illustrate the text of the Pledge of Allegiance.

Red, White and Blue: The Story of the American Flag
by John Herman (Grosset & Dunlap, 1998).
Describes the history of the United States flag, including how it has changed over the years and what it symbolizes.

Flag Day Fun

1 Flag Day is June 14. On what day of the month is your birthday? Color the boxes to make a pattern.

	before the 14th	on the 14th	after the 14th
Pattern of Boxes	**AB/AB pattern**	**AAB/AAB pattern**	**ABC/ABC pattern**

2 Have you ever celebrated Flag Day? Draw blue circles on the left side of the flag.

	yes	no	I'm not sure.
Number of Circles	**fewer than 3**	**exactly 3**	**more than 3 but less than 6**

3 What is the first letter of your name? Draw green triangles in the middle of the flag.

	A to M	N to Z
Number of Triangles	**odd number less than 4**	**even number less than 5**

4 What is your favorite color? Draw red squares on the right side of the flag.

	red or orange	yellow or blue	green or purple	another color
Number of Squares	**1**	**2**	**3**	**4**

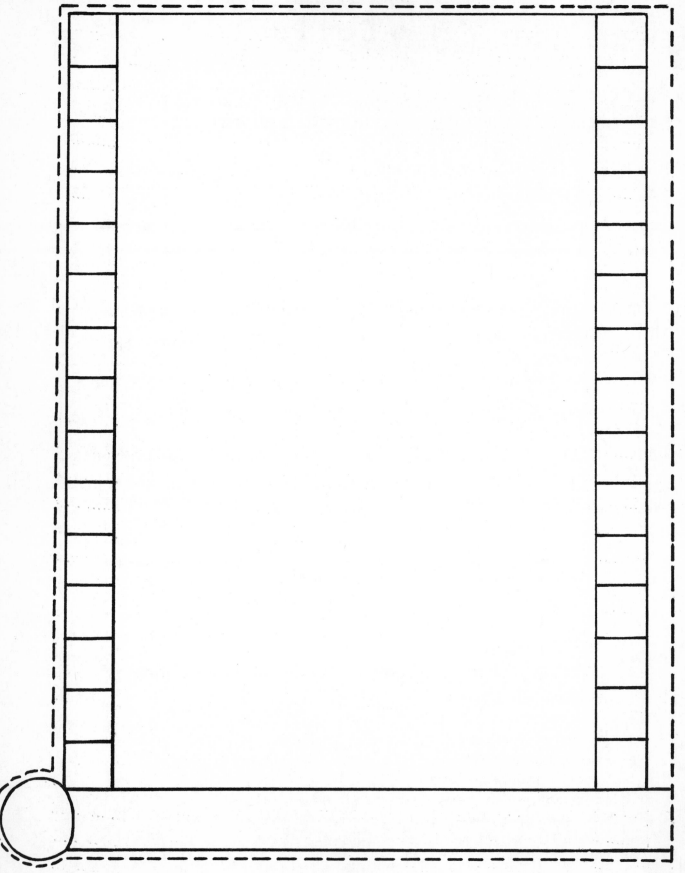

Pack Your Suitcase!

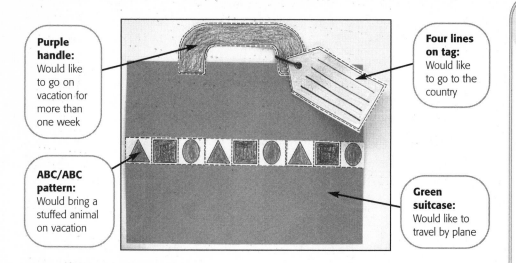

Purple handle: Would like to go on vacation for more than one week

Four lines on tag: Would like to go to the country

ABC/ABC pattern: Would bring a stuffed animal on vacation

Green suitcase: Would like to travel by plane

Creating the Glyph

1. Distribute copies of the suitcase glyph patterns and legend to students. Review the legend, one characteristic at a time, as you display a glyph you have completed. Then distribute the other materials, and invite students to use the legend to create their own personal suitcase glyph.

2. For question 1, have students choose the color of construction paper that corresponds to their answer. Have them position the paper horizontally and glue the handle to the top of the suitcase.

3. After students have completed question 4, punch a hole in the tag. Then help students attach the tag to their suitcase with yarn.

Critical Thinking

Ask students to guess where most students would rather go on a vacation. Then ask students how they could find the actual answer, using their completed suitcase glyphs. Once students present their ideas, suggest that they group their glyphs by the number of lines on the tag. Explain that each group represents the place students would most like to take a vacation. Have them count and compare the number of glyphs in each group to find out which place is the top choice. Then have them predict which place most students in another class would prefer to take a vacation. Have students poll the other class and then compare the results to their predictions.

Math Skills

- greater than, less than, equal to
- geometry: shapes
- patterns
- time concepts: seasons of the year
- counting
- one-to-one correspondence

Materials

- reproducible glyph patterns and legend (pages 59–60)
- completed suitcase glyph
- 9- by 12-inch blue, green, red, orange, and yellow construction paper
- scissors
- glue or paste
- crayons
- pieces of yarn cut to 6 inches

Explore More

Math, Social Studies   Display a large United States map with a mileage key. Help students search the map to find their state. Draw an X to mark your school's city or town (approximate if needed). Then invite students to name other places on the map that they would like to visit. Each time, write the name of the place on chart paper. Ask a student to measure the distance between that place and the school's location, using a length of yarn. Then have the student compare the length of the yarn to the mileage key to find the distance in miles. Write the distance next to the name of the place on the chart. After each student has had a turn to name and measure the distance to a different location, ask the class to compare the distances on the chart.

Language Arts, Art   Have students create a travel brochure for a place they have visited or would like to visit. Invite them to use a variety of collage materials to create their brochures. Have students share their projects with the class, then display the brochures in your reading center along with a collection of travel books.

Science, Social Studies   Invite students to choose a place they would like to visit for the first time. Have them research this place to learn about the climate. Encourage them to describe the climate and the type of clothing they would pack for a visit there. What other items would they pack? What kinds of activities would they do there? After sharing, have students write a story about their imaginary vacation.

Literature Links

The Bag I'm Taking to Grandma's
by Shirley Neitzel
(Greenwillow, 1995).
This picture-book rebus features a young boy who packs all the important things in a bag to take to Grandma's: his baseball mitt, toy cars, space shuttle, toy animals, cuddly bunny, pillow, book, and a flashlight.

I'm Taking a Trip on My Train
by Shirley Neitzel (Greenwillow, 1999).
Readers hop aboard an imaginary train with a young boy in this story told in cumulative verse and rebuses.

Ira Sleeps Over
by Bernard Waber (Houghton Mifflin, 1972).
Ira's excitement over spending the night at Reggie's house turns to worry when his sister asks whether he should take his teddy bear.

Pack Your Suitcase!

1 How would you like to travel on vacation?

	by car	by plane	by boat	by train	another way
Color of Suitcase	blue	green	red	orange	yellow

2 How long would you like to go on vacation?

	less than one week	exactly one week	more than one week
Color of Handle	black	brown	purple

3 What would you bring on vacation? Glue shapes to create a pattern.

	a game	a book	a stuffed animal	something else
Pattern on Suitcase	AB/AB pattern	ABB/ABB pattern	ABC/ABC pattern	ABA/ABA pattern

4 Where would you rather go on vacation? Draw horizontal lines on the tag.

	to the beach	to a city	to the country	to another place
Number of Lines on Tag	2 lines	3 lines	4 lines	5 lines

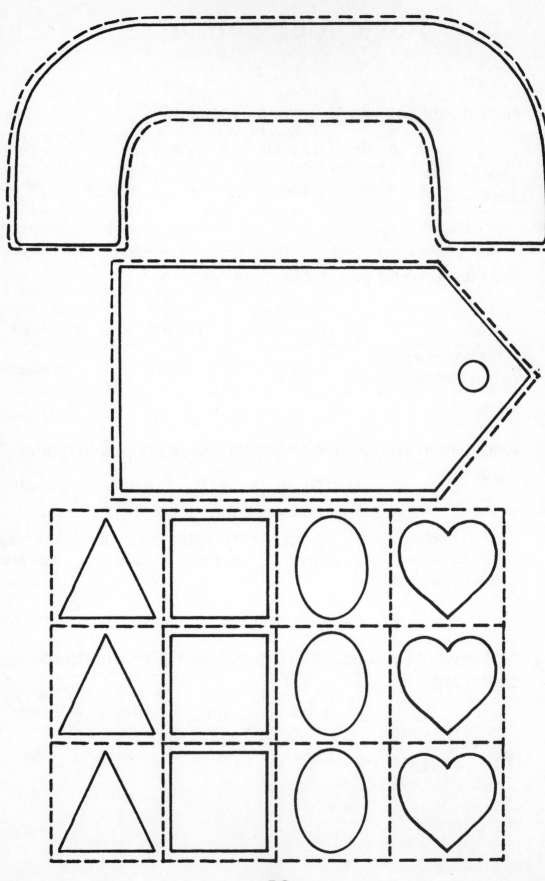

Summer's Here!

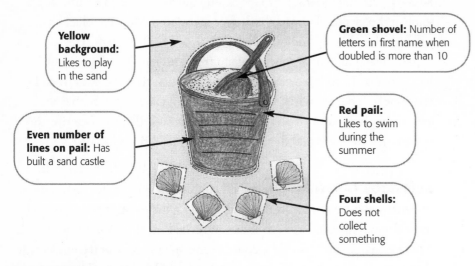

Yellow background: Likes to play in the sand

Green shovel: Number of letters in first name when doubled is more than 10

Even number of lines on pail: Has built a sand castle

Red pail: Likes to swim during the summer

Four shells: Does not collect something

Math Skills

- counting
- one-to-one correspondence
- odd and even numbers
- geometry: horizontal lines
- greater than, less than, equal to
- simple multiplication

Creating the Glyph

1. Distribute copies of the sand pail glyph pattern and legend to students. Review the legend, one characteristic at a time, as you display a glyph you have completed. Then distribute the other materials, and invite students to use the legend to create their own personal sand pail glyph.

2. For question 1, have students choose a color of construction paper that corresponds to their answer. Have students position the paper vertically and glue the pail and shells onto it.

Critical Thinking

Have students count the number of lines on each pail and record this number on a sticky note attached to the glyph. Challenge students to think of ways to group the glyphs by the number of lines—for example, from greatest number of lines to fewest or from fewest to greatest. Ask students to think of a way to group the glyphs that would help them analyze the data on it. Lead them to the understanding that grouping by odd number of lines and even number of lines shows whether students have ever built a sand castle. Then have students interpret data on specific glyphs. Ask questions such as:

- Does the student with the greatest number of lines have a collection?
- How many students have built a sand castle and have more than 10 letters in their name?

Materials

- reproducible glyph patterns and legend (pages 63–64)
- completed sand pail glyph
- 9- by 12-inch yellow and orange construction paper
- scissors
- crayons
- glue or paste

Explore More

Math   Challenge small groups of students to create patterns using some of the glyphs. They might do this by color of pail (red, blue, blue, red, blue, blue) or by number of lines (1, 3, 5, 7). They might create patterns using more than one attribute (red pail, red shovel, blue pail, blue shovel). Then have other groups of students study the pattern and continue it. The group that created the pattern can assess whether the pattern has been continued correctly. Encourage students to describe the pattern first in words and then using letters (AB/AB, and so on).

Science, Math   Create a sand center in your classroom and give students a chance to play in the sand! Cover a table with newspaper and place damp sand in a large tub. Bring in several small containers in different shapes, such as cubes, cones, rectangular prisms, and cylinders. In the center, draw pictures of each solid shape and label them. Have students visit the center in pairs and use the containers as molds to create sand shapes, just as they would using a sand pail to build a sand castle. Have students use the pictures to identify the shapes they are creating.

Language Arts   Give students several story starters to inspire summertime tales, such as:

- I was playing at the park, when suddenly my dad shouted, "Look over there! It's . . ."
- I thought it was the beginning of another ordinary summer, but I was wrong. First, . . .

Encourage students to write an outline to plan the beginning, middle, and end of their stories. When you're ready to celebrate the beginning of summer, invite a few students to share their stories each day.

Literature Links

All You Need for a Beach
by Alice Schertle (Silver Whistle, 2004).
Rhyming text describes a day of fun.

Sand Castle
by Brenda Shannon Yee (Greenwillow, 1999).
Working together produces wonderful results—
a spectacular sand castle!

Sea, Sand, Me!
by Patricia Hubbell
(HarperCollins, 2001).
Upbeat verse tells all about fun at the beach.

Summer's Here!

1 Do you like to play in the sand?

	yes	no
Color of Background	yellow	orange

2 Have you ever built a sand castle? Draw horizontal lines on the pail.

	yes	no
Number of Lines on Pail	even number	odd number

3 What do you like to do during the summer?

	swim	go to the playground	ride bikes	another activity
Color of Pail	red	blue	green	purple

4 Double the number of letters in your first name. How many letters are there?

	fewer than 10 letters	exactly 10 letters	more than 10 letters
Color of Shovel	red	blue	green

5 Some people collect shells. Do you collect something?

	yes	no
Number of Shells	2 or fewer	more than 2 but fewer than 5

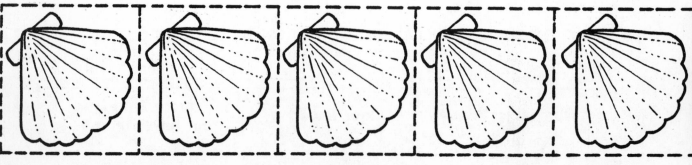

Great Glyphs: Holidays & Seasons   Scholastic Teaching Resources